A Visit to an Automobile Factory

D. M. Rice

Table of Contents

Going to the Factory

One morning my dad woke me up early.

"Surprise!" he said. "You are coming to work with me."

My friend
Angie →

My dad has
the best job
ever. He works
in an automobile
factory. They
make cars there.

Did you know?
Automobile is another
word for car.

Engineers

My dad is an engineer. That means he helps to plan how a car will look and work.

Dad works with other engineers. They work together so the car will be safe and run great.

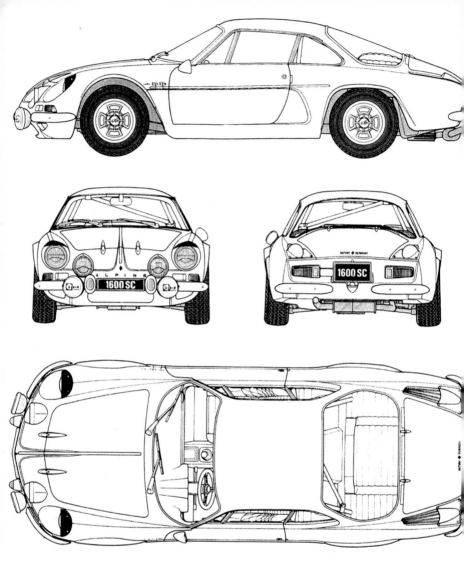

Dad and his team draw
their plans. They look like
this.

I want to be an engineer,
too. So, I draw my own plans.

When the plans are ready, the car can be built. But first, factory workers must make or buy all the parts for the car. There are hundreds of parts!

A car needs springs, brakes, and a steering wheel. It needs pistons, valves, and more.

It is not easy to build a car!

Assembly

Once they have the parts, workers can put the car together. This is called assembly.

They work in teams. Each team builds a different part of

the car. One team builds the
engine. Another builds the
body. Another is in charge of
the wheels and tires.

There are many teams
with many different jobs.
All of them are important.

Each team checks its work
carefully. They want the

people who drive the car to be safe.

Engineers check the work, too.

Ready for Sale

When the cars are ready, they go to a shipping yard. The shipping yard sends them to dealers. Sometimes the cars go by boat. Sometimes they go by truck. Then people buy the cars from the dealers.

When I see cars on the road, I feel proud of my dad. He makes good cars for people to enjoy.

When I grow up, I'm going to work at the automobile factory, too!

How a Car Is Made

How is a car made?
This chart will show you.

 Plans are drawn for a new car.

 Parts are made for the car.

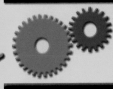 The car is put together by teams.

 The car is checked and tested.

 The finished car is sent to the shipping yard.

 The shipping yard sends the car to a dealer.

 People buy the car from the dealer.

19

Glossary

assembly

automobile

dealer

engineer

shipping yard